Landslide

Poor Management and how to avoid it

Landslide: Poor Management and how to avoid it

Eric Kasten

Copyright © 2016 by Eric A. Kasten

ALL RIGHTS RESERVED

Cover design by Therese Joanis

To my parents and my wife, thank you for all your support.

Contents

Introduction 9

Chapter 1: Setting expectations 14

Chapter 2: Perception vs. Reality 23

Chapter 3: Priorities 28

Chapter 4: Implementing change 33

Chapter 5: Walk the walk, don't just talk the talk 39

Chapter 6: Efficient employees 45

Chapter 7: Cause vs. Symptom 49

Chapter 8: Management triangle 56

Chapter 9: Conflict with manager 61

Chapter 10: Poor performance 65

Chapter 11: Performance Ratings 70

Chapter 12: Summary 75

Introduction

The purpose of this Book is to bridge the gap between managers and employees. It examines both the manager's actions and the employee's subsequent reactions to give a clearer view of the message being sent by the manager and how it is being received by the manager's direct reports. Real world examples are used to illustrate important points in each chapter. The examples were all personally witnessed by the author. However, names and details have been changed to protect the innocent.

After having been on the receiving end of both effective and "not-so-good" managers for many years I can now provide a portfolio of positive managerial character traits as well as a list of tactics that did not work. I'm the type of person who witnesses poor management and says "I can do better than that", so I studied for and received a degree in business management. If one pays attention to effective managers, one can learn a lot. You also can learn just as much from less-effective managers (only think the opposite impact).

So what I'm trying to say is "Yes!", there are very good and very poor managers out there. You probably already knew that. What most managers have in common is that they intend well, but don't realize that they're contributing to a negative work environment. Just remember, it's never too late to turn things around. Employees want the team to succeed; this is the same thing a manager wants. We all have the same goal.

For the last 20+ years I've had workplace highs and lows in a technical field. I'm not going to say I've seen it all, but I'm confident that I've seen my fair share of both greatness and miserable failure. In the following chapters I will share these experiences with you and address both sides of the situation (management and employee). I will discuss how to get the most out of your team. The intent is for each chapter to give you something to think about.

In this handbook I will refer to the "receiver" of messages as a direct report (DR). The direct report is the "doer" or can sometimes be a low level manager. I will refer to the "transmitter" of messages as a manager (MGR). The manager is the one transmitting the direction, or issuing the orders, to the direct reports in order to achieve a corporate goal. When using "employee", I am referring to both managers and direct reports equally.

So, what is management then? What do managers do? Let's explore... A manager takes a corporate goal or direction and translates it into tasks and goals for his direct reports. A manager sets parameters and expectations for his team. The manager also provides guidance to his team members and performs all the associated administration duties. It sounds simple on paper, but is difficult in practice because we are all individuals.

Each team member has individual motivations, desires, expertise, etc... that makes influencing them to focus on the same goal somewhat difficult. There's no single "magic bullet" for everyone. All employees are motivated by money, but they are motivated to varying degrees by money. Employees are also motivated by challenges, but again, to varying degrees. The most common factor among most direct reports is the adverse impact that negative management can have on them. A poor management style can have a greater negative impact on team members than a good management style can have positive impact, in other words... movement in the positive direction is taken in baby steps, while movement in the negative direction is taken in land-slides.

Read all the motivational books you can. They're great. But, avoiding de-motivational actions is even better!

Chapter 1: Setting expectations

Expectations can be stated directly, or they can be implied through actions. Saying that a report should be provided to the manager every Monday is a clear expectation set by the manager. If the manager focuses on a specific metric within that Monday report, places emphasis on improving that metric, and takes action to improve that metric, there is an implied expectation that that metric is important and the direct reports should be focused on achieving that metric... without additional words being spoken. On the other side of that coin, the manager is lowering expectations on the other metrics by not emphasizing their importance as well.

There are many ways a manager can set an expectation without even knowing it. For example, high performers may appear to have more time on their hands than lower performers. Lower performers may appear busier as they struggle to manage their workload. Should a high performer be rewarded by offloading work from the lower performer onto the high performer or should the high performer be rewarded by allowing them to enjoy any slack time they earned? These are two opposing solutions and there are more solutions closer to the middle, but considering these two solutions, what is the expectation being set by the manager if one or the other solution is used?

Let's say you're in a team meeting and you hear the following conversation.

Conversation 1:

MGR: "Starting Thanksgiving, John, I need you to start ordering equipment for Marcy because she is overwhelmed."

1 week after thanksgiving…

MGR: "Why isn't the equipment column updated on the tracker spreadsheet? Marcy's sites are missing. You should be doing this for each piece of equipment you order."

John: "Oh, I didn't know I was supposed to do that for Marcy's sites too. I'll get it."

2 weeks later…

MGR: "Why aren't the new equipment orders on my weekly report?"

John: "I didn't know I had to include them."

MGR: "Come on, you're a smart guy. You should know to include them on the weekly."

John: "Ok. I'll make sure to include them going forward. Are there any other requirements I need to be aware of?"

Several points are quickly noted in this example. First, the manager failed to clearly set expectations. As a deliverer of messages, the manager has first responsibility to set the primary expectation and to include any sub-expectation associated with it. Is John to only place orders for Marcy, or is he to fully own the orders trough their lifecycle?

Second, John assumed his new responsibility was limited to only ordering equipment. As the receiver of the message, the direct report has the responsibility to ask for additional clarification. When id doubt, John should either ask his manager or work with Marcy to make sure all aspects are covered.

Third, if workloads are the same, but John is a high performer and Marcy is struggling with her workload what is the expectation being set? Is the holiday season causing a temporary increase in orders requiring Marcy to be busier? Is Marcy unable to manager her workload or is there an underlying training issue? Lastly, is Marcy gaining a form of reward for being behind, and is John receiving a form of punishment for being more efficient? The last question needs to be examined because long term, high performers who perceive they are punished with more work will no longer be motivated to perform at a higher level.

How could the manager have handled this situation better?

By initially setting a small, simple expectation and then expanding the expectation each week, John loses his sense of security in what he is doing; he also loses focus on the task as it increases beyond initial expectations. In project management, this is known as scope creep. The scope starts out defined within certain specifications, but over time the scope slowly increases. It's not a terrible thing, but it does not build manager support, especially when clarity of task or purpose is a recurring issue. As a manager, every action should have the intent of building the support of the direct reports. Not only is the manager's support important when goals change, but it also helps motivate through consistency and strength.

It's like saying, "John, go clean the bathroom". After

John is finished to the level he thinks is expected, the manager says "Why didn't you clean behind the mirror?". John thinks "Why didn't you tell me that upfront?", but says, "ok, no problem." On the next bathroom, John cleans behind the mirror, but this time the manager says, "Hey, you didn't scrub under the plunger in the sink". The expectation needs to be defined.

Delivery of the message is important as well. Wording, content, clarity and sincerity all affect how a message is received. Compare "John, you've completed all your work for the week. Help Marcy finish hers." vs. "John, you've done a great job getting your work completed ahead of schedule. I would appreciate it if you worked with Marcy to help her as well." Consciousness of one's delivery goes a long way in management/employee relations. The second option is positive. It sends the signal that John is respected and for John to share some of his best practices with Marcy.

In the conversation above, the manager asks why

something wasn't done as if the direct report knew he was expected to do it. The manager could have taken a better route and taken responsibility for the lack of clarity. Instead of "Come on, you're a smart guy. You should know to include them on the weekly.", consider "Oh, okay. I should have clarified that better. Going forward make sure you update the weekly." The second option is better isn't it? It resolves the situation, without placing blame on the employee.

One of the best ways to provide clarity of expectation is to provide meeting notes after a meeting or to provide a written statement of expectations after a conversation. I know; meeting notes are a Management 101 item, but more often than not, they're overlooked. Some employees may also send an email to their manager outlining their perception of the expectations. This is acceptable, but may not always be well received by some managers. If you, as a manager, receive these notes from a direct report, encourage this follow up. Also, make note to provide that same level of clarity yourself next time. It may be the employee's way of expressing concern over expectations.

A fundamental necessity when providing clear expectations and sub-expectations is that the manager must have the understanding and knowledge of the task in order to set the expectations. If the manager lacks this understanding and knowledge, discuss it with the direct reports. An open discussion will reveal what the manager needs to know and allows the direct reports to bring up any questions or concerns they may have before a problem arises. Lack of knowledge is not a weakness unless it is kept hidden.

Employee to employee communication should include enough information for the receiving employee to start making progress right away. Replying to an email in order to request more information is a time waster. Be aware of the information the recipient will need to get the job done and provide that information the first time. Anticipate the expectation of the recipient. Information hoarders may think they're creating job security, but in reality they're only creating frustration.

Be clear and include all the details.

Conversation 2:

MGR: "You need to get this rating up from 63% to a minimum 95% for the monthly report card. And you need to do it by the end of this month. If you need to make a few bucket categories and assign everything to there, that's fine."

DR: Summarizes the expectation, "Do everything necessary to get measurement to 95%, including the bucket approach. Ok."

Next month...

MGR: "95% was good enough yesterday. We need to be at 98.5% minimum now. By the way, thanks."

Next month...

MGR: "Since the minimum is 98.5%, we need to be at

least 99% to accommodate any "dips" in the numbers."

So what's happening here? It is a changing target month over month right? Sure. But, take a look at the last month's marching orders. Goal is 98.5%, but you have to get 99%. In the previous 2 months the goal was the goal. Also, in the first month the improvement was from 63% to 95%. That's a big improvement and probably included all the "low hanging fruit" (I know it did because that's how we met that challenge).

After 95%, the next goals were 98.5% and then 99%. Not a problem, but there was no discussion between management and direct reports on how to achieve those numbers. "Just do it" was the directive. There was no direction on 'how' to achieve those goals, but for the sake of discussion, let's examine how it could have happened.

If the manager had discussed with the direct reports (via two-way dialogue) on ways to achieve these goals, two things would have happened. First, the manager would have created "buy-in" from the direct reports. Buy-in always increases motivation, but it also helps set expectations due to the conversation leading up to buy-in. A discussion would help the manager better equipped with knowledge for discussing what happened if the goals were not achieved, as well as discussion of future setting of goals. Secondly, the direct reports would receive more information concerning the options for goal attainment. The direct report who understands the mechanics behind the metric is better equipped to execute the orders. The mechanics of the measurement not only create understanding, but also help the direct report focus their efforts on the tasks that have a direct impact on meeting the expectations set by the manager.

Could the manager have done a better job smoothing out the progression from 63% to 95%? Possibly this was out of his control. The goals may have been provided to the manager in the same way it was provided to the direct report. But, also possibly, the manager could have influenced the improvement schedule before it was delivered to the direct reports. The manager could have set expectations with his/her superior for a smoother improvement schedule.

Similar to Conversation 1, this example presents a changing expectation. The business world is full of moving targets, but it's the manager's job to 'normalize' the expectations as best as he can. Managers should not drop a bomb on the direct reports and then run for cover. If a 'number improvement' project comes down the pipe, managers should strategize with the direct reports on how to achieve the expectations presented. It should always be a team effort. If necessary, the manager should get involved to accomplish the goal by assuming limited responsibilities as well… depending on the scenario.

Clear expectations go a long way in team motivation. Setting expectations is more involved than simply saying to do something. Expectations can cause angst when not clearly defined and can undermine management on future endeavors when a pattern of unclear expectations emerge. Clear expectations help identify what direct reports will work on and help optimize their time and reduce duplicate work.

Chapter 2: Perception vs. Reality

What is perception and what is reality? Good question. I've been told perception is reality. But, that's ridiculous. Perception is someone's internal image of someone or something and that perception could be based on anything. It is a 'virtual reality' if you will. Reality is something that exists as a fact. So how can perception be reality? If you are currently using this saying… stop now!

A manager who has a perception of someone or something has the responsibility to find out what the reality is. A manager should never operate on perception. Personal bias is difficult to suppress, but perception is easy to correct or confirm.

A manager also has to be able to identify a direct report's perception and correct that perception if incorrect. Part of identifying perceptions is being open to questions or discussions initiated by the direct report and to the direct report's concern. The direct report's responsibility is to be transparent with their perceptions and to seek the truth.

Conversation 3:

MGR: "Perception is reality. You need to change people's perception of you. I know that you are working eight hours, but some people have the perception that you don't. You should start working later so you change that perception."

DR: "But you know that I get my work done and I work my eight hours. Can't you just tell them it's all good?"

MGR: "I can't change their perception of you. You have to do that yourself."

So in the office, perception exists in someone's mind. Yes, it's based on one's own observation of events and conversations, but rarely does someone always have the whole picture. Since perceptions exist in one's mind, how is an individual supposed to know what another person's perceptions are? Therefore, how can someone change what they do not know? Taking this one step further, should an individual be focused on the perception of others, or should that individual focus on reality and doing their job?

Contemplate that for a few seconds… 5…4…3…2…1…

People should focus on reality and their job. If one has a negative perception of someone else, it is his/her responsibility to clarify that perception. If one does not take the initiative to clarify one's own perceptions, one does not deserve to have input about others. Rumors get started from erroneous perceptions and offices become vile, backstabbing, demoralizing places. Encourage and focus on reality. As a manager, discourage the reliance on perceptions and rumors will be reduced.

If you focus on your job and reality you can't go wrong. This is true for both managers and direct reports. Of course, make sure your manager knows what you do and query them about what's on their mind. If you think your manager's perception is not favorable, then definitely clear that up. Be transparent with each other. But if your manager does have negative perceptions and is not working to clear them up him/her self, then you should be looking for new opportunities as this is a clear sign of a weak manager.

There's a saying that says something like "You can only change yourself, not others". It is true. You can only change yourself. You can not change anyone else. If you try, you'll end up a failure because you'll get nothing done.

As a manager, encourage the pursuit of reality. Encourage direct reports to change what they have the power to change. Do not listen to perceptions. If a manager is aware of incorrect perceptions, the manager should correct those perceptions.

Conversation 4:

MGR: "I know you're very busy. But, you need to stay in the office later."

DR: "Is there something I'm not getting done? As far as I know I'm ahead of my workload."

MGR: "Reality or not, the perception is that you don't work enough. If you want my support to be a manager yourself, you need to show me that you're willing to stay late."

DR: "So, you want me to stay late for the sake of staying late?"

MGR: "Yes."

Great conversation isn't it? And very real. There's no work-related reason to stay late and it can be a waste of resources. What is the direct report expected to do, twiddle his thumbs? The manager offers no reason to stay late except it is felt to be important for the direct report to be seen at the desk at later hours. Not very productive. Also, the manager made no attempt to support the direct report. The manager should have informed others of the direct report's efficiency accomplishing tasks as well as the fact that the direct report was indeed working the required hours.

For more on efficiency, see Chapter 6.

What would you do as the manager in this example? Do you think the above conversation would have a negative or positive affect on the direct report? How would it affect the short term and long term performance of the direct report?

Perception is a dangerous thing. Both positive and negative perceptions can mislead. Nobody can fully understand another person's perception. As humans, we can even have wrong perceptions about ourselves. Reality can only be determined by facts, measurement and completed events. Perceptions are more qualitative while reality is quantitative.

Chapter 3: Priorities

A manager is responsibility for knowing what his direct reports are working on and setting priorities for these tasks. There should be a team environment with a clearly defined leader (preferably the manager). Priorities can be communicated with direct words, establishing a weighting system for tasks, or by having a clearly defined priority list. When leadership does not set clear goals, contradictory marching orders and chaos occur.

What if an Army General gave each of his officers certain goals and left them to their own devices to accomplish these goals? The officers would not know which goal is most important for achieving victory. They would not know which goal should be completed first. They would likely lose the war.

Conversation 5:

DR: "Yes, I have a question. I'm already working on projects A, B and C. What priority should I give to this new project D?"

MGR: "Everything is top priority. Everything has to get done equally."

DR: "But, isn't something more important than the rest? What should I focus on first?"

MGR: "Focus on everything."

As a manager, if you don't know the answer, admit it. Direct reports can smell indecisiveness oozing from a manager's pores. Admit it and discuss the projects in question. When the direct reports understand the driving factors behind their tasks they can help the manager identify which tasks are more important, easier to achieve, or what may take longer to achieve. All of these can play a role in setting a priority.

Conversation five provides no priority of goals. The manager is effectively isolating himself and may not know enough to make the decision himself. What's going to happen when the direct report fails to complete one of the projects on time?

The direct report is left to prioritize the work himself. This may be effective, but what are the odds that the direct report knows all the background information on these projects needed to make the best decision on his own? The manager should at a minimum discuss the pros and cons with the direct reports and establish some sort of hierarchy of tasks. What is the manager's role and purpose in the organization if he can not prioritize goals?

Of the four projects being worked on by the employee in the example, at least one must have more importance than another. They can not all be top priority. Deadlines, exposure to customers and executives, and business impact can all help set priorities. Even if the manager does not have enough information to make the decision, he should ask questions and explore the expertise of the direct reports to find some sort of project prioritization.

What does the manager do if he does not know what priorities to set for his direct reports? What would you do if you did not know? What can you do to gain the needed information? There is ownership at both the manager level and the direct report level when it comes to determining priorities.

Contradicting priorities have no place in a manager/direct report relationship. Consistency is the key to smooth, continuous task completion. One also sets the stage for future endeavors by being consistent. Once a consistent precedent is set by a manager, the direct reports require less direction in the future. On the other hand, if there is a history of contradicting directives, the direct reports will require more direction in the future. The goal of consistency is to make work easier for the manager as well as the direct reports.

How can one remove contradictions and increase consistency? One way is to keep meeting notes and review them as needed. Some effort in reviewing the notes is required, but this is effective for jogging memory. Another way is to have a discussion with direct reports about issues instead of dictating "how it's going to be". This method keeps everything transparent through discussion. It also removes the manager's directive which can be the cause of contradiction. One needs to find what works for himself. Most importantly, one needs to make the effort to remove contradictory directives.

What is the effect of setting the wrong priority? As an example, the President of the United States has a lot on his plate and many initiatives to prioritize. Does he always prioritize correctly? No. He prioritizes as best he can with the information he has, and according to the direction he wants to take the country. If he gets new information, or he needs to make a course correction, he re-prioritizes. Re-prioritization is an acceptable activity so long as it is not a frequent activity.

Don't be afraid to re-prioritize, just don't do it in a vacuum. It's ok to prioritize with conditions as long as those conditions are known. For example, "Right now, your priority is project B first, followed by project A. If the report next week shows low numbers then project A will take priority over project B. So, stay on your toes." Be upfront and transparent.

Chapter 4: Implementing change

Sorry, no example conversations in this section. Just an exploration of change processes. Let's compare two ways to implement change… quickly pull off the band-aid, versus implementing change slowly.

'Pull off the band-aid' version… This is the process of implementing a change between one day to the next. For example, "As of Jan 12th, the old ordering process will not be used. Instead we will be using the new ordering process." How does this work and what are the pros and cons?

Pro: This process leaves little, or no, time for resistance

to surface. There's no time for negativity to infect and spread through the direct reports.

Con: This process requires all, or close to all, training be completed prior to the deadline. It requires a short learning curve for the employees so it should be executed during a slow time in the business. It could also lead to mistakes due to lack of experience and slow response times.

Pro: It demonstrates strong leadership by upper management. A corporate decision has been made and that's the direction the company is going.

Con: If a strong plan is not in place and risk assessments are not identified, the transition pain can be extended longer than needed.

Implementing change slowly version… This process spreads the transition period over a long period of time and usually involves incremental steps through the transition process. It is sometimes better to use this process for a very large change by cutting the single change into smaller changes. How does this work and what are the pros and cons?

Pro: Reduces a large disruptive change into smaller less disruptive changes.

Con: Spreads out the change over a longer period of time, which may cause more disruption if it overlaps a busy time for the company.

Pro: Easier for a less effective management team to implement because the changes are smaller.

Con: Allows more time for negative dissent to exist and grow. Resistance to change, using this process, is more common and needs to be accounted for.

Whichever process is used to implement change, there is one common denominator… it has to come from the top.

Upper management must support the change and must back it up with its actions (walk the walk, don't just talk the talk… see Chapter 5). Without 100% backing by management the change will be at risk. Management is in place to lead. Change requires leadership.

An employee committee may be necessary to help the transition process, but upper management must not put the change process in the hands of the direct reports. If this occurs, the transition will not succeed because management support will not be present. The change will be coming from the bottom up. If a single direct report is tasked with accomplishing a change, the direct report must be given adequate authority to accomplish the change. Adequate authority means being able to make decisions for management and to instruct management on what to do. It also means, if expectations are not met, the appropriate manager, or team, is held accountable for not meeting expectations. If a single direct report is tasked with this, then he/she should be fully vetted by management first.

Implementing change, when done right, provides motivation to the direct reports. It shows growth and a desire to adapt to new things. Change is often resisted at first, but often ends with success. To end with success, management must embrace the change and take ownership of the change process. When management embraces change, the direct reports follow the manager's lead.

Which of the below two examples show strong leadership? Which example leaves direct reports de-motivated?

Example 1: A company distributed new software for all employees. Upper management instructed everyone to begin using the new software, but never enforced its use. Management did not embrace the new software either. Ten years later, and several versions of the software later, only one department was using the software and there was still resistance to using it within management.

(A true story.)

Example 2: A company initiated a new organizational structure. It was implemented in steps, beginning with upper management. Starting at the top, upper management was restructured over a period of several months. The subsequent lower level of management was then restructured, followed by the next lower level. This was done until the restructuring reached all employees. During the process, responsibilities were changed. Responsibility changes were made by upper management and communicated down to the employees. In just a couple months the entire organization (thousands of employees) was restructured.

(Another true story.)

Chapter 5: Walk the walk, don't just talk the talk

This goes for direct reports as well as managers. But the focus is on managers due to their position in the leadership structure.

You've probably heard the expression "Do what I say, not what I do". This means people pay attention to the actions of those around them and they compare those actions against their words. If someone says, "don't cross the road", but they them self cross the road, they are setting a precedent to cross the road. They are also undermining themselves the next time they say to do or not do something. Their expectation may contradict the expectations of the direct reports.

Conversation 6:

MGR: "You can only work from home if you have an emergency. There will be no scheduled "work from home" days."

Later that day via email…

MGR: "I will be working from home tomorrow."

Be aware of the example being set. Direct reports have a long memory when they feel slighted. Maybe an emergency came up and the manager had to work from home the next day. If so, this must be communicated, especially after making the statement "You can only work from home if you have an emergency." In this example, the manager is causing a negative impact to their working relationship. The only way to rebuild the relationship is with time.

Be aware of the signals you are sending to your direct reports. Negative signals take a long time to overcome. It takes many more positive signals to overcome a single negative signal. So if you send a few negative signals, it's going to be a long time to get back to neutral.

Conversation 7:

MGR: "From now on, I need two weeks notice, minimum, to schedule vacation days."

Later that week via email…

MGR: "I'm taking a vacation day tomorrow. John will be standing in for me."

Yes, this actually happened. …Do as I say, not as I do… sound familiar? How do direct reports interpret this manager's actions? When instances like the above happen over and over it grows resentment in the direct reports. Words and actions have to match. They matter.

Where does distrust of management come from? Was it the manager's strategy to set one rule for his direct reports when no rule or different rules apply to him?

Conversation 8:

MGR: "I'm looking to you guys for ideas and input. If you have concerns you should bring them to me." ...He then described "constructive dissent" as a policy.

DR makes suggestions regarding roles and responsibilities, and brings concerns to manager.

MGR consistently turned down all suggestions and labeled certain DRs 'combative' for discussing and supporting opposing ideas.

As a result of the manager's request for ideas and input, a direct report was actually written up for following the 'constructive dissent" policy encouraged by the manager. Is this good for employee morale? If the direct report was out of line, perhaps instructions on how to dissent constructively could have been shared by the manager. If the request for constructive dissent is made, the manager must be capable of coping with the responses.

Managers must set the example. If a manager says "Do not accept meals from vendors", then goes out to lunch with a vendor, this tells the direct reports that it's ultimately ok. It tells the direct report that the manager is just telling them what company policy says, but it's ok to break that rule.

A manager should live by the standards expected of his direct reports. Actions speak louder than words. Saying one thing and doing the opposite sends the message that what was done is okay regardless of what was said. Managers should promote "Do as I do", which means management needs to live up to its own expectations.

Conversely, a "do as I say, not as I do" environment causes the manager's words to carry little weight. It further causes employees to disregard a manager's direction whenever it is convenient. The manager loses control of the team and loses respect as the leader. Ultimately, the manager makes himself an outsider to the team.

How does one avoid this?

Instead of placing specific guidelines on a team, a manager should give some leeway to the team in general. The more guidelines and rules set by a manager, the more chance there is for the manager to contradict his own rules and guidelines. Treat each situation individually, not by placing overall rules on the team. If a direct report shows himself to constantly need attention, address the situation with that employee. Don't let one bad apple cause you to throw out the entire bushel of apples.

Are you being overwhelmed by direct reports requesting vacation days? Is it summer time? Is it unseasonably warm outside? Is there any reason why they shouldn't take vacation days? Is there any work that will suffer if they're on vacation? Encourage them to schedule their vacation ahead of time, but accept the fact that exact dates may change.

Chapter 6: Efficient employees

What is your definition of an efficient employee? Is it an employee who is physically in a seat 8 hours? Is it a cheery employee? Is it the one that over analyzes everything? Is it the one that gets the most done, but with mistakes? To that end, how do you measure efficiency?

There is no perfect employee. The employee that operates well in one environment may not operate well in another environment. One manager may consider employee X the most efficient, but another manager may consider employee Y the most efficient. Quantitative measurement is the only sure way to know for sure, but it doesn't take "environment" into account.

Decide what traits you consider to be the most efficient and share these traits with your direct reports. Direct reports need to know what your expectations are. Encourage efficiency because efficiency lets you accomplish more with the same resources. Don't punish an efficient direct report by making him stay later just to be seen. Don't punish an efficient direct report by making him pick up the slack for a non-efficient employee either. Ask the direct report what new challenges would motivate them. Challenge and encourage the efficient direct report. He may be ready to move up to the next level within the company. He may have time saving processes that should be shared with his co-workers.

Efficient direct reports often use processes that increase their efficiency. Have these direct reports share their secrets with their peers. Find ways for the more efficient direct reports to influence the less efficient ones. Set the same expectations for all direct reports so that the less efficient are pushed to find their own efficiencies. Add additional challenges and expectations to the more efficient so they do not become bored. But, don not allow the additional challenges and expectations to become a penalty for efficiency.

Making efficient direct reports constantly pick up the slack for less efficient peers is inappropriate. Doing this occasionally is acceptable. Having to do it on a consistent basis indicates the less efficient direct report may be overburdened, may be under performing, etc… As a manager you must assess the situation and address the less efficient direct report's lack of work completion. Do not "dumb down" the entire team to the lowest common denominator just to avoid taking corrective action on that lowest common denominator. Also, make sure to provide honest praise when praise is due.

Efficiency is a double edged sword. It must be encouraged and gains must be made. If a direct report becomes very efficient, he can become 'locked' into his job because he does it so well. The direct report may be the subject matter expert, in which case, it is difficult to let that person step away. However, the direct report may want to move on from his current position to another one. If this is the case, don't allow him to be held back. What will happen when you start holding someone back? They may end up leaving the company entirely.

Don't let efficiency become a burden to the direct report.

Chapter 7: Cause vs. Symptom

What is the "cause" that creates a "symptom"? Think of it as a "cause" and "effect"...

Conversation 9:

MGR: "Some of you have exceeded the $50 per day meal expense when you were away on training. From now on if you come close to $50 per day, I will not approve your expense report."

Because of previous conflict, direct reports did not feel welcome to ask questions regarding the manager's policy and left the meeting not knowing how close they can come to $50. They also are no more educated on the company's travel expense policy.

In the above conversation, what is the cause of the changed policy and what is the symptom? What new, unclear process was created?

Most likely, lack of knowledge was the cause. Maybe the employee that exceeded $50 intended to pay the difference. We don't know because there was no inquiry into that. The Manager jumped the gun. The cause was exceeding $50 per day in expenses. The manager addressed the symptom, which was exceeding the $50 limit on expenses. Had the manager dug into the symptom to discover the cause, it may have turned out to be a lack of knowledge about the policy. Also, it was only one direct report, yet the entire team was punished. Finding the cause of a problem is the correct course of action.

In this example the manager created a new 'cause' which will lead to new symptoms by not setting clear expectations (see chapter 1). A clear expectation would have been, "Don't exceed $48." This isn't the best course of action, but is still better than what actually took place. "Close to $50" is too ambiguous.

Sometimes the cause is not so easy to identify. When this is the case, the manager needs to dig deeper and work with his team to identify the root cause. It may not be easy and the results may not be favorable. But, it must be done. Without resolving the cause, the symptoms will continue to appear. You can swat flies all day long, but until you close the front door, you'll never get rid of the flies.

How do you get to the root cause of a symptom? Ask questions. Open the floor to discussion. Don't stifle an open discussion. As a manager you may assume to know what the cause is, but there may be an underlying issue that you're not aware of. Maybe the direct report's spouse is in the hospital and this is affecting his work performance. It never hurts to engage a direct report with questions. A good way to set the foundation before a meeting is to jot down 3-4 questions to ask regarding your symptom. This prepares you in advance to start the questioning process.

Two-way communication is the key. Not only is communication key to finding the root cause(s), but is also necessary for effective team building. Communication allows a manager to explore presented options, discover unknown options and engage direct reports in the issue. Sometimes it is necessary to guide the conversation so that the direct reports discover the cause on their own. This leads to allowing the direct reports to develop their own solution as well. This is not weak management. In fact, empowering direct reports is a reflection of strong management.

For anyone familiar with troubleshooting basics, there are logical steps to follow when looking for an underlying cause.

The first step is elimination. Eliminate possibilities of

the cause to reduce the scope. Anything you can do to end up with a narrower scope will aid the decision process and optimize any discussions. Hopefully you will end up with a handful of "culprits" after the elimination step.

Second is ranking. Rank the remaining possible causes from simplest to most difficult. 'Most likely to least likely' works too if you have enough information to do that. Either way, there should be a prioritized list when you're done.

Third is, make a change. Only one change at a time. If you make more than one change, the true cause will not be known. After making that one change, observe the results. Is the problem fixed? If not, go to the next item on the list and repeat.

This is a simplified description of troubleshooting, but it fits here because it applies to cause and effect. It provides a method of identifying an unknown cause.

What happens when this troubleshooting method is applied to Conversation 9?

What possible causes can we initially eliminate? How about:

-Travel policy changed between time of travel and time of expense reporting.

-Direct reports didn't know how much they spent.

Next, prioritize any remaining causes. Order them from most likely, to least likely.

-1 Direct reports did not know the travel policy.

-2 Direct reports planned to repay the difference of expenditures above $50.

-3 Direct reports tried to defraud the system.

Make one change and observe…

Share and discuss the company's travel policy with the team. Make sure everyone understands the policy and its limitations. Now, observe the outcome. If the direct reports continue to exceed $50 and are not covering the costs above $50 per day, then additional steps may be necessary.

The above list was prioritized that way on purpose. If number 2 (repay the difference) had been first, it would have included the same information as number 1 (don't know the travel policies) when covering costs over $50 was discussed.

The take away here is to focus on the cause. Don't focus on symptoms because you'll never get to the end of that road.

Chapter 8: Management triangle

Many times there is a disconnect between upper management and direct reports concerning the definition of an "ideal manager". Looking up the chain of command, direct reports view knowledgeable, involved managers as the best. Looking down the chain of command, some upper management may lean toward managers that are hands-off, and believe that managers do not need to understand the jobs that their direct reports perform on a daily basis. A manager that is involved in daily tasks is sometimes known as a subject matter expert (SME). The SME manager takes on the roles and responsibilities of the direct reports under him. What is best? ...A manager that is hands off? ...Or a manager that is a subject matter expert?

Odds are each has his/her place depending on the situation. There are teams that are very self sufficient and a less hands-on manager could be very effective. There are also teams that may be new or are experiencing problems and could benefit from a more hands-on/knowledgeable manager.

A third type of manager is one that has acquired a high level of respect from the direct reports. This management type may, or may not have a thorough background in the subject matter of the direct reports. This manager succeeds through respect. That respect translates into authority. Because of this authority the respected manager accomplishes tasks. Managers can also earn respect from their direct reports. This respect allows a manager to do more than just accomplish tasks. Respect allows managers to create efficiencies, and to get more out of the direct reports.

A manager can operate without respect from the direct

reports, but this leads to less productivity and usually lower moral. An elected official leads may have been elected due to respect from the voters but they initially manage their direct reports using authority until they have earned their respect.

The best managers provide a balance between three categories: hands-off management, SME management and respect management. This is the management triangle.

From the direct report's perspective, respect for a manager is important. Without respect for a manager, the manager's effectiveness suffers as well as morale of the direct reports. When the manager is respected he can accomplish more with his employees and achieve higher goals and efficiencies. It's not that direct reports purposely go out of their way to sabotage a manager; it's just that their heart isn't in doing the job to the best of their ability. Morale brings the heart into the equation.

If one is promoting individuals from within, respect is

very important because one is likely to already have a relationship between direct reports and the new manager. Any existing conflict between these individuals is immediately amplified. It is a little different when an external manager is hired because this new manager starts with a high respect level, it is then up to this new manager to build on the respect, or undermine himself.

In environments where managers carry high levels of respect, performance increases and metrics improve. Direct reports trust the manager to make the best decision. When issues arise that the direct reports dislike, creates more work or affects them negatively, the direct reports respond better. Think of it as a bank that the manager is saving up his earned respect in. When needed, the manager can withdraw some of that respect and apply it to the situation. This is why it is good to constantly be building mode as a manager. Constantly building respect, positive relationships, communication and respect yields results when issues arise.

Hands-off managers often do not comprehend what the direct reports do day-to-day and are therefore at a disadvantage. They rely on their direct reports to decide what needs to be done and how to do it. They also rely on the direct reports to make critical decisions. The manager can not educate the direct reports on new technology so training becomes a bigger concern when new technology is involved. Rather than being "hands-off", the manager should spend his time taking "reporting" and "administration" activities from the direct report's workload. Not only does this draw the manager into being more involved in what is being accomplished, it also allows the direct reports to spend more time managing their work.

A hands-off manager can also be quite successful if he trusts and empowers the direct reports. If there is no two way trust, then a hands-off manager will not succeed.

Subject Matter Expert managers end up being quite involved in the workings of the team. These managers have less time to send reports to upper management and are more likely to be overloaded and behind on their work. Direct reports can learn a lot from these managers, but not in the area of management. Subject matter expert managers often lack the willingness to delegate responsibilities, but if they do delegate, they stay quite involved.

Respect managers get things done through their higher level of influence over the direct reports. They may have varying levels of SME skills or hands-off management skills.

So what is the best balance for a manager? The answer is decided by the organization and the requirements of the position. Ideally it's a specific balance between the three types. You need to find what works best in your organization.

Sometimes one is put in a position that requires one of the three areas to be stronger, but that may be a weak area for the manager. If you are aware of this yourself... First, I commend you for recognizing an area of weakness. Second, what can you do to overcome that weakness? Can you increase the other two areas to compensate? Is training available? It's most important that you work to improve the weak area. Your direct reports will see that you are trying and should support you. Just don't do nothing and expect others to change for you.

Chapter 9: Conflict with manager

Conflict is not a manager reprimanding a direct report for poor performance. It is a personal difference that creates a tear within the team. Conflict between manager and direct report is never good. Conflict between a manager and direct report not only degrades that relationship, but also negatively affects the other team members.

When a direct report questions a manager, finesse is required. This questioning should be encouraged. It brings both sides together and together they are enabled to move forward. Direct reports who do not question unclear, illogical, non-business-as-usual directives do so at their own peril because they are responsible for not achieving or following those directives.

Managers who take a defensive position when questioned by their direct reports reflect a lack of confidence and leadership. They lose the bond they have with their team. It also has a long term negative effect on direct reports who may hesitate to speak up about legitimate concerns in the future.

Conflict needs to be addressed immediately and directly between the involved parties. Managers who respond to a conflict with an individual by emailing and setting new rules for the entire team end up undermining themselves. Keep conflict and conflict resolution contained to only those involved and resolve the issue immediately. Do not use your authoritative power as manager unless absolutely necessary. Work it out as two professionals.

If the conflict stems from severe personal differences

then clear guidelines must be provided to the direct report to avoid future conflicts. Sometimes people need to agree to disagree. Sometimes the direct report may need to look at other employment options.

Conflict can stem from a direct personal remark or an off-handed, terse comment...

Conversation 10:

DR: in first team meeting with a new manager: "Since you asked what we need, I can tell you we need someone who can back us up and not be a 'yes man' and let the other departments off load their work into our group."

MGR: "Calling me a yes man is like calling me the "N" word."

Yes, that's an actual dialogue that took place in a team meeting. The direct report even reported it to Human Resources. Human Resources said it was not an issue and left it alone. But, it set the stage for future conflict between the manager and that direct report ... all in front of the team.

Had Human Resources stepped in and negotiated the conflict it could have been resolved and never brought up again. Had the manager realized what he said and corrected himself it could have been resolved right away. But instead, it became a festering sore that caused the employee to reject much of what the new manager tried to implement. It also caused the team, as a whole, to question the manager and his initiatives. The manager himself became even more defensive and less tolerant of the employees' actions. Things became worse before they got better.

Chapter 10: Poor performance

It's the snowball effect! As soon as it becomes acceptable for a direct report to perform at a sub-par level others take notice. Once this happens two results can occur...

Occurrence 1: Other direct reports will take advantage of the situation and their performance will drop to a sub-par level. A new, lower, level of expectations will be set for the team. Some direct reports will take advantage of this by lowering their performance to meet the new minimum.

Direct reports falling into this first category are likely to be individuals who are low to average performers to begin with.

Occurrence 2: Other direct reports will take note of how little their peer is getting accomplished and become upset. They will be upset about how much they're getting done versus how little their peer is getting done. Their inner disgust will slowly build over time and may be shared with the manager. It will definitely be shared with their peers and become a "water cooler" topic.

Direct reports falling into this second category are likely to be individuals who are above average to high performers.

Either effect is not limited to the involved team and is likely to spread to other teams as well. When poor performance is not addressed, the effect spreads quickly and to a larger audience than expected.

What to do?

Have a discussion with the direct report. Always address poor performance right away, and directly with the low performer in question. The poor performer needs to know that their manager is aware of their performance and is displeased. Talk to the direct report about expectations, but don't insult them. Motivate them.

Only if approached by another direct report, should the manager mention performance corrections to a poor performer's peer. But, if approached, be honest. Let them know you're doing something about it. Just don't share details. Honesty here is the best answer. If you're approached it is because others have noticed the poor performer. A firm response will assure them this is being addressed. It also indicates how future issues will be resolved. They'll know it is not tolerated.

What if a direct report continues to perform at a sub-par level? First, consult your code of business conduct handbook or Human Resource department for your course of action. Most importantly, don't let it go. Don't let it grow into a morale eating beast that negatively impacts the entire team and possibly other teams.

In regard to rewarding good performance, use rewards wisely. Make sure they are sincerely valued by the direct report. A highly valued reward will tend to cause more resentment among the non-winners than a less valued reward. However, even a less-valued reward will have a negative affect on non-winners over time. Sometimes the best reward is a simple, sincere thank you from management. Regardless of the value, the reward should be earned and not just handed out in order to hand it out.

Issuing rewards can be a difficult balancing act. It all depends on the professionalism of the direct reports, the job function of each team member and other factors. Make sure that when rewards are given, they are presented sincerely and honestly. Rewards should not be cheapened in any way. If cheapened, they lose value. Never reward a direct report for simply doing their job. Remember, for many, performance is personal. If someone is rewarded for simply doing their job, or if a reward is misrepresented, damage will be done to the reward system and to the motivation of others.

Recognition from upper management carries a lot of weight and is often coveted. However, if mistakes are made when rewarding employees much damage can be done. One example is omitting a team member from a team reward.

Tossing out low value trinkets in a meeting is fun that everyone can enjoy. Be it raffle style or rewarding correct answers to questions, everyone likes to get coffee cups or other things. And for those that don't win, there's always the next meeting.

Chapter 11: Performance Ratings

If you want to build a strong, motivated team, do not rate performance on a bell curve or forced ranking system. Instead, rate direct reports against equal, consistent expectations. Remove subjectivity and embrace quantified measurements. And, make sure you communicate those expectations to the entire team at the beginning of the rating period.

The problem with rating against a bell curve or forced ranking system is that no matter how hard everyone works, some one is going to get an abnormally low rating. This is not always justified. Sometimes everyone on a team is a high performer and management has to accept that. A fair, measurable way to provide ratings must be used. Bell curves and forced ranking are subjective rating systems that undermine motivation.

Bell curves and forced rankings pit direct reports against one another. This is not conducive to team building. It becomes team deconstruction. If direct reports know that no matter what, one of them is going to get a sub-par performance rating, they could no longer function as a team. Instead they will be individually working to make themselves look better and to make others look worse. This kind of environment will encourage back-stabbing.

By equally rating employees against known expectations, inadequate performance is easily identifiable and a low, or high, rating is justifiable. Equal expectations are the means to providing fair, measurable ratings for all direct reports. Used effectively, fair, measurable ratings can lead to improved performance in lower performing direct reports.

Many companies provide mid-year and end-of-year ratings. This is a great way to make course corrections. It also ensures that end-of-year performance ratings are not a surprise. Communicating performance status to direct reports twice a year should be a minimum! Performance issues should be communicated from manager to direct report(s) whenever they occur... immediately. Don't lock it up and bring it out at a mid-year or end-of-year performance review. By then it's too late to correct the issue, and the employee may resent the inability to correct the issue prior to the review.

If a direct report has corrected a performance issue prior to a review, don't use that against him. It's fair to mention the issue and that it was resolved, but don't use it to justify a lower rating. Let the direct report be rewarded for correcting the issue. This is motivation! This is positive reinforcement!

As a manager you need to recognize positive actions

and encourage them. Everyone makes mistakes. Accepting that and recognizing direct report's efforts to correct mistakes is the difference between a great, motivational manager and a lack-luster, mediocre manager. Learning from mistakes is a normal thing. Remember, the purpose of communicating performance issues is to provide the direct report an opportunity to make performance corrections. Corrections are not reward worthy in and of themselves, but they should be acknowledged and encouraged.

Unless a performance issue becomes a recurring one, put it in the past and forget about it once it is resolved. If one constantly brings up an issue from a previous year, that manager is being petty. Not only does one make it impossible for the direct report to move on, the direct report is also being held back. You're taking away the opportunity for the direct report to improve himself.

360 degree feedback asks direct reports to provide a performance review of one's peers. This is a useless tool. It

can promote baseless criticism by peers. It also can remove open communication within a team. Some places use 360 degree feedback to gain feedback from direct reports about their manager. This is a poor tool for that purpose. Either direct reports will not trust the system and be hesitant to provide honest feedback about their own manager, or they will go overboard in emphasizing issues. Another drawback to 360 degree feedback is that it doesn't allow the subject of negativity to defend themselves because it's based on subjectivity. A manager should be strong enough, involved enough and empowered enough to review his own direct reports.

Chapter 12: Summary

Management is an art that takes effort, desire and skill. It comes naturally to some, while others can work at it for years and never feel successful. What works in one organization likely won't work in another organization. Managers have to adapt to each situation quickly.

What you should take away from this handbook:

1. Set clear expectations. Patiently answer questions to clarify any issues. As expectations change, be clear and upfront about them. If you failed to set clear expectations, admit it and rectify the situation.

2. If you have a negative perception it's up to you validate that perception. If you hear a negative perception about a direct report you must introduce reality. Perception is not reality.

3. Set clear consistent individual goals that lead to a common goal. Do not establish contradicting priorities. Be aware of your message.

4. Decide on the best method for implementing change. Make sure clear upper management support exists or it's doomed to fail.

5. Practice what you preach. Don't just talk the talk, walk the walk. You'll get more mileage out of your message and your employees. Contradictions are noticed and remembered.

6. Clearly define what you consider vital in an efficient employee and encourage efficiency. Give employees the tools they need to be efficient.

7. Identify the symptom, but treat the cause. In fact, eradicate the cause. Don't waste time or resources on a symptom.

8. Realize the skills required to be the best manager you can

be in the eyes of others. The best manager is a balance between being involved and hands-off, being a subject matter expert and strictly managing. The manager must also build the respect of his direct reports.

9. Do not allow personal conflicts to exist between manager and employee. It undermines the effectiveness of the entire team.
10. Address poor performance immediately. Never let sub-par performance become acceptable. Don't allow a reward to be cheapened. Sometimes a sincere thank you is the best.
11. Performance ratings must be based on equal expectations. Bell curves and forced ranking systems deteriorate the team environment.

There you go. This was a quick and dirty little book to guide managers toward a fruitful and rewarding experience, while identifying the common pitfalls that should be avoided. Direct reports will appreciate your efforts to create a positive environment and to increase motivation. Avoid negativity!

www.ingramcontent.com/pod-product-compliance
Lightning Source LLC
Chambersburg PA
CBHW070109210526
45170CB00013B/798